Cryptocurrency Investing in the Age of Dollar Chaos

Table of Contents

Why Am I Not a Millionaire 4
Understanding Market Manipulation Is Real 17
We Are Living Science Fiction Plot Lines Now 27
Less Analog Cash Means More Risk 40
Banks No Longer Have a Value Proposition.................................... 50
US Markets No Longer Offer Price Discovery 55
Is Tim Cooke Starting a Rollerball League 60
SEC Objects to Rollerball League... 67
Jack Ma's Rollerball Team... 71
Who Else Might Have Rollerball Plans... 75
The Rollerball Cryptocurrency Hypothesis 79
Jeff Bezos Saves the Republic.. 89
Cryptocurrency Investing is an Oxymoron 96
Diving In and Getting a Hardware Wallet...................................... 103
Cryptocurrency Concerns 113
Appendix: Specific Cryptocurrencies... 118
    Bitcoin 118
    Ethereum.. 120
    Litecoin 121
    Dogecoin.. 123
    Monero... 126

Why Am I Not a Millionaire

The first question one asks the author of a book like this is, "Why are you not a millionaire if you know so much?" which is a valid question. There is no need for me to dodge it or "doge" it as the case may be.

I have been working in the tech space almost my entire working life. I have gone from keypunch cards to blockchain with a whole lot in between. There were surely some opportunities to become a millionaire. Somehow I managed to avoid the burden of millions of dollars though.

I do not know if I am particularly proud of this accomplishment. Given my economic situation calling it an "accomplishment" probably not the appropriate appellation. After all, men like Jeff Bezos and Elon Musk are coders who turned their skills into BILLIONS. Bill Gates and Mark Zuckerberg are other examples of what the bank accounts of long-time coders should look like.

I have made some mistakes that cost me quite a bit of money over the years. I am not proud of being stupid or misguided, but mistakes are how one learns. I am still here and my bank accounts are not empty. I do feel like I have learned a lot from my mistakes.

I feel a bit of an obligation to share how I managed to avoid the burden of having millions of dollars. After all, I must have made some serious mistakes to not be a millionaire given my long career in tech. Without a doubt I did make mistakes.

Some of my mistakes have been painful and bring with them real regret. Dealing with regrets can be difficult. It is good to seek advice and consider the advice, but there is a limit. You have to be the one who makes the decisions. Always understand this power and burden. Always embrace this power of choosing. You make the decisions about how you run your life and spend your money.

By making sure you embrace this personal obligation of choice, you own your decisions. Owning your decisions makes the regrets easier to deal with, but they are still painful as regrets can be. I am a person who has made some mistakes.

I can live with those mistakes because I never turned over decision-making to anyone. Anything I did, I did because I decided it was the right thing. Admittedly, it might have been a poor and emotional reason. Whatever might have driven any given decision of mine, they were always mine.

This book is full of advice about how I am modeling future events to help make life and money decisions. It is just that though. It is just advice. You need to make the decisions. You need to decide how this model of future events applies to you and your situation. Maybe these ideas and models are wrong. Time will tell.

My models and ideas are based upon a long arc of experience in computers and tech. Not just as a project manager or business analyst but as an actual coder for nearly forty years. I am still coding today and do not plan on stopping. It has helped me gain the insights which will follow.

When I first started, I was young and arrogant. I was doing far more work than my compatriots at the first corporate job I landed. I had become good at the position. I wanted to be paid for being more productive.

Corporate salary structures are not always very flexible. I was stymied. I was frustrated and I quit suddenly on Halloween of 1992.

I was quite frustrated with the bureaucracy. I ended up cashing out of the employee profit-sharing plan before being fully vested. I retained NO holdings at the company I had spent six years at. A year later, the company was bought by a private capital firm. The $10,000.00 I walked away with would have been worth $250,000.00 had I waited a mere 365 days to pull the trigger on quitting.

Ouch, but we do what we do. That was thirty years ago. I try not to imagine what a quarter-million dollars would be worth to me thirty years later. I deal with the regret because I own the fact I threw a temper tantrum and quit a good job. Then afterward, I still did not control my emotions enough to recognize the value of the stock I held but instead cashed out in a fit of anger. Dumb? Yep, but nobody told me to do it. I did it.

It made me try harder at the next position I found myself in. I learned quite a lot about business at the next job and kept my emotions in check much better. I rose to be the general manager of a small medical software company in four years. When the owner sold the company, the buyers did not need two general managers. I moved on.

I left with so much knowledge I started a small consulting firm. I got certified to send electronic claims to Medicare and Blue Shield. I could handle any other insurance companies through a clearinghouse API. I was set to make money because insurance companies paid for claims delivered electronically in the late stages of the twentieth century.

I had seen good products go nowhere without salespeople to do the dog and pony show. I knew I was not good with people or dog and pony shows. My father-in-law was though. He sold health insurance. I moved down to Southern California to be closer and push the business.

Unfortunately, before much could happen, he died. It was a terrible time. My mother-in-law's financial situation was not great. I had a wife and a young child and now a mother-in-law whose financial situation was sketchy. I had not planned on staying in Southern

California, but I decided I should for a little while. A little while turned into quite a long time. The electronic claims opportunity passed as the 21st century dawned.

It was a real missed opportunity, I admit, but I felt the best thing for my family at the time was for me to make money as quickly as possible. Booting up a new business does not allow for that. I do not feel much regret on this one, even though it represents a missed opportunity to be a millionaire.

There are several times after this where I chose to leave a company so I could spend more time with my children. I regularly negotiated four ten-hour day weeks. I took Wednesdays off to the surprise of some. I was able to walk my children to school once a week. I was able to run a chess club at the elementary school for a few years too. I also coached many soccer teams because I had negotiated a work schedule that allowed me to do so.

More than once, I sat down at the "annual review" and negotiated four ten-hour days INSTEAD of a pay raise. It was that important to me. I wanted to spend time with my family. I wanted to coach my sons' soccer teams. I decided what it was I wanted, and it was not more money.

I have one more little regret I should share, which is probably the biggest reason this book is getting written. In 2011, I started researching digital currencies because my sons told me about video game ecosystems. I began to realize digital goods could be commodities. I then stumbled onto Bitcoin while researching other digital commodities.

It was going for about one dollar! I started to buy some. I had entered everything into a checkout screen but had not clicked the final send for the transaction on my credit card. Right at that moment, the CTO of the company I was working for came up and asked for status on a project. Oops! I dropped out of that browser tab right quick.

I had a good status to report. It was no big deal because I had decent progress to show him. He went away satisfied. However, the "checkout session" had expired. I would have to jump through all the hoops again to get to the point where I was about to buy 100 bitcoins. And you know I had a thought. I said to myself, "You know

Tony, this seems like a good way to evaporate $100.00." Maybe fate had smiled upon me and saved me a C-note, I assured myself. I did not go back to the site for three years.

Do I regret that choice? Yes, I guess I do, but it was mine. I could have chosen differently. I could have chosen to surf digital currencies on my home computer and not on company time, but I did not do that. I did what I did. I decided what to do next. I decided. I was the decision-maker.

Even though I decided not to buy in 2011, I still kept an eye on Bitcoin. The price went up and down and all around after my aborted purchase. In 2012 and going into 2013, the price really shot up. It went well over $1000 and stayed there. It did not take long to figure out why. The sovereign debt crisis in Europe was in full swing, with Greece leading the way downward.

Consequently, it affected another European nation closely tied to Greece, Cyprus. Citizens of Cyprus got hit hard. The terms to bail out the nation were harsh. To the average Cypriot, it felt like their **bank account has been raided by another country's government.**

The deal to bail out Cyprus had been strict. Just like that, $1 in every $16 of your supposedly safe money is gone. If you're wealthy enough to have more savings, it could be $1 in $10. That became the new reality facing bank depositors in Cyprus.

The German Central Bank came to the rescue, but there was a price. Cyprus had to pick up some of the cost. It could not afford much, but the Germans were determined to get something back. There had to be consequences for Cypriot behavior.

The terms of the Cypriot bailout were shocking. Germany coughed up about $13 billion, and, in exchange, Cyprus levied a "one-time" tax on bank deposits to raise an additional $7.5 billion. This tax took 6.75 percent from insured deposits of €100,000 or less and 9.9 percent from uninsured amounts above €100,000. Depositors got bank stock equal to whatever they lose from the tax.

If you're wondering why anybody kept their money in a Cypriot bank, well, they didn't. It became an open invitation for an old-fashioned run on their banks, so the banks were closed. An extended holiday was declared and the average Cypriot suffered. There were big foreign depositors trapped in Cyprus too. It was seen as a tax haven for many well-off Russians.

The European Central bank instituted very tight controls on the banking systems in Cyprus. People were allowed minimal access to their money for some time. Bitcoin's price began to rise. It broke through one thousand and kept going. I understood the Bitcoin use case better now. Rich people were not going to allow Bitcoin to die.

The Bitcoin use case allowed rich people access to their money. The original backers of Mark Zuckerberg, the Winklevoss twins, jumped in with both feet. The Winklevii have been Bitcoin evangelists ever since. The sovereign debt crisis in Europe cemented the Bitcoin use case for the world's rich and powerful.

The 21st century had already seen the United States ratcheting up the financial sanctions in the name of reducing terrorists financing their evil agendas. If they caught a few tax evaders in the process, so be it. The United States being the owner of the world's reserve currency has been a powerful foreign policy tool. Financial sanctions really could bite with the computerization of money in the late 20th century. It even brought the great tax haven of Switzerland to heel.

The Cypriot banking crisis demonstrated the extent of control the banks had over the systems which moved money. The banks in conjunction with the sovereign nation-states were in control. More than ever before due to the 20th century computerization of all things money. The control was near absolute.

This made the Bitcoin use case clearer for anyone seeking to get away from the dollar's hegemony. The wealthy needed an alternative to a system which had become too tightly controlled by nation states and their geopolitical machinations.

When financial markets settled down in 2014 and Bitcoin dropped below one thousand dollars again, I bought in finally. I have kept my finger on the pulse of crypto ever since. Now over seven years later, I think I have gained some real knowledge of cryptocurrencies. It is one reason I was waiting at the station when the Dogecoin train came by.

The money world is in turmoil now. There is no good regulation. Money is in flux, but power remains power. Power must be denominated in something. What that "something" is going to be remains unclear.

In 2021, I have made and lost a quarter-million dollars in a hundred days. It has been hard to cope with such wild swings in the crypto portfolio. However, I cut myself a little slack since one has to make decisions on little data these days. In any case, I decided I was holding or HODLing, as they say in the crypto world.

Cryptocurrencies will provide opportunities for making money. Options for making lots of money will present themselves over the years I suspect. Dogecoin has been good to me and threatened to push me into the millionaire class. This book is about why this oldster became a hodler.

Because health and my family mean so much more than money, it has made it easier to HODL through this craziness. I remind myself repeatedly, one dogecoin is worth one dogecoin and the other valuations are subject to change. At the time of this writing, I remain a simple thousandaire, but surfing this Dogecoin Disruption could give me a lift.

Understanding Market Manipulation Is Real

Honestly, I have not been all that great as a retail investor. I tried to follow a rational plan. I tried to make investment decisions based on sound historical principles. The principles governing market dynamics in a traditional supply and demand economy have been largely worked. They are boring. They require patience and a long view to succeed, but they have been historically successful.

Back in the nineties, I thought I knew something. As the Dow Jones blew past 6,000 mid-decade, I said to myself, this kind of upward spike has to level off. Around this time, Alan Greenspan famously commented on the "irrational exuberance" in the markets. The Dow Jones rocketed through 7,000 and then 8,000 in 1997. I felt it simply could not continue and made my investment decisions accordingly. However, it did continue well into the 21st-century.

I heartily agreed with Greenspan's assessment. My agreement led me to to lose a ton of money on gold stocks. The irrational exuberance continued much longer than anyone expected. I probably should have paid a little more attention to Keynes. The economist John Maynard Keynes once said, "The stock market can remain irrational longer than you can remain solvent."

I listened to pundits who claimed the way to participate in the market, as well as hedge against a possible downturn, was with gold stocks. Unfortunately, this turned out to be inferior advice. If I had bought physical gold, I would have been better off, but stocks can go to zero. When gold prices plummeted, many of these mining companies went out of business. I was left with zeroes on many of my bearish investments entering the new century.

By the time the market finally sputtered with the dotcom flame-out, all of my bear positions were completely wiped out. It took over four years for the house of cards built on irrational exuberance to come crashing down right after 2000. It did not matter that I had eventually been proven right. I had bad timing. My gold stocks were worth zero before the market crashed, so they could not recover any value the way a roll of gold coins did. Bad market timing is costly. Keynes truth became mine.

"The stock market can remain irrational longer than you can remain solvent." ~John Maynard Keynes

Unless one has deep enough pockets to survive manipulations of the market, fundamentals do not matter. If enough money and power line up on one side of a position, it is tough to swim upstream against it. Don't fight the Fed became the mantra of all investors, including me, in the new century.

After I had recovered my economic wherewithal and nerve from the losses of the nineties, I stayed in the markets. I was all in, 100% invested in equities during the beginning of this century. I ignored the price of gold even as it finally began to recover.

The aughties were a halcyon time of easy money and high employment. Some of my clients started to slow pay me in late 2007. I even saw a couple go out of business going into 2008, leaving me with uncollected accounts receivable. Little did I know how bad 2008 would become.

The fact big money and power seemed to be pushing the market up had made me a lackadaisical portfolio manager. I figured I was staying in no matter what. Why pay attention and drive myself crazy. I thought I was brave when I was actually stupid.

Not paying attention caused many of my assets to shrink significantly during the Great Recession. It was a terrible time. I will always recall the 2008 Christmas as one of particular stress and sadness for me. Things were very tight. The only income my wife and two young sons had was ME! I wondered how I would make it. I made it through somehow. I learned there was a high price to ignoring investments.

We managed to save the house as my wife rebooted her career. A decade after the Great Recession, we were solid, if not rich. Having made it through, I realized I needed to pay very close attention to my investing and savings. I needed to steer the financial boat. I needed to keep at the tiller and be ready. It meant doing constant course recalculations without necessarily changing course, so I was sure were still going in the right direction.

Staying at the tiller of the financial boat was one of the big reasons I paid attention to cryptocurrencies. The financial storms I had weathered so far taught me one big lesson, the wealthy survive. The wealthy are often well-positioned before these things happen. Where are the wealthy putting money was something I researched regularly. Where might the wealthy put their money in the future became an important thing to try to figure out.

The stock market still seemed to be the place to go at the beginning of this century despite the rocky years of 2008-2009. Ultimately, the stock market would eventually return the truth still seemed true. It was still an article of faith for me and everyone else. It still felt like price discovery was extant in the American markets.

The Trump presidency brought a lot more clarity to the market. There was no way this president's policies would not exacerbate the boom/bust cycle inherent in all markets. I moved a good deal of money to the sidelines, because Trump seemed to be pumping a market which was long in the tooth. I moved to about 50% cash near the market tops of 2018 expecting a downturn to come eventually. I was quite smug in December of 2018 as for once my predictions seemed correct.

However, Trump was not going to let the market go down. He began to flog Fed Chairman Powell to release more money into the markets. There was no good economic reason to do this as the time to tighten monetary policy is during economic expansions. Once Powell relented and actually cut interest rates, the markets started to "melt-up" in 2019. My smugness was replaced by an intense FOMO and regret. (*FOMO: fear of missing out*)

The beginning of 2019 felt like the nineties. It was different though, because back then there was a lot more "slop" in the system. Entering the nineties, coming out of the tight monetary policies of the eighties, there were cash surpluses. My experience in the nineties taught me "irrational exuberance" can continue for years even if the numbers do not quite add up. I could see the central banks of the world were stoking the 2019 exuberance with cheap money. Market truths were obscured by a tsunami of dollars.

With the central banks participating and negative interest rates occurring, it was hard not to be worried. Keynes had taught me it was possible for irrationality to continue for a few more years. There were too many entities needing loose policies to finance their debt loads. I told myself, "It will continue to go up until it does not."

It was hard to say everything was rosy in 2019 when the repurchase market required so much intervention from the Federal Reserve. The reaction of the market to normal tightening was extreme in late 2018. To those in power, the 2018 market downturn justified juicing the markets. To those who had bet on normal central bank behavior and responsible action, we felt a little cheated in 2019. We had done the right thing, but the central bank had done the politically expedient thing.

In late 2018, we saw the Federal Reserve show itself as no longer an independent entity. The Federal Reserve cut rates during an economic expansion! The markets started to "melt-up" in 2019 due to Powell's cheap money regimen. The Trump administration cheered Jerome Powell's actions. Frankly, everyone was happy EXCEPT bond holders with Jerome's cuts.

Since Jerome Powell's obvious capitulation, his statements have become increasingly irrelevant. Everyone can see what is going on. There is only one path for the Federal Reserve. That path is to suppress interest rates for as long as they can.

For years now, the Federal Reserve has been under-reporting inflation. **It now seems clear the Federal Reserve knows inflation is coming. The Federal Reserve also knows there is nothing they can do about it. The Federal Reserve has no bullets in its gun.**

Jerome Powell keeps talking about full employment and assuring of the central bank's altruistic desire to facilitate money printing for the people. Since when is the central bank's role to ensure everyone has a job? This sounds suspiciously like the old Soviet Union. Nothing is more illustrative of the strange new world of 21st century economics than for Western bankers to sound like communists.

We know Jerome Powell is NOT a communist. He is a man in a terrible position. A man who knows the future is out of his control. Jerome Powell is delivering a narrative to prepare for the future. It is really because the Federal Reserve is such a compassionate institution that it will ALLOW inflation to "*…run a little hot.*"

Such statements presumes the Fed has some control, which has become laughable. The Federal Reserve delivered a "skewed narrative" for why inflation has been so low for so long because it justified suppressing interest rates. They had no choice given the level of debt, so they under measured and told everyone what they wanted to hear.

The prognostications from the Federal Reserve are there to serve a high inflation future. He is implicitly explaining why inflation is not going to be in the control of the Federal Reserve. He is explaining why they are going to sit back and do nothing. He is prepping everyone for why they will "...*let it run hot...*", WHEN THEY SHOULD tamp it down. Jerome Powell knows he cannot control whatever inflation comes, so he delivers this narrative of compassion as a future fig leaf.

Jerome Powell is spinning a story about why America should sit back, and hope things settle down when inflation hits. This story was always about making it sound real and there was some control. In the end, it has made Jerome Powell sound like a communist. He isn't. He is just a very scared man.

Frankly, we should all be scared at this point. The economy is no longer being properly managed. There will be consequences. This book's ideas can help you prepare.

We Are Living Science Fiction Plot Lines Now

The world has begun to change so significantly the old ideas just do not seem to apply. I am kind of guessing about where to make "play" in the market, but not exactly. Instead, as I realized how much things were changing, I began to engage in some inductive reasoning. I began riding the ideas I had gleaned from science fiction plotlines years ago. I realized these ideas were becoming useful in making predictions.

In my youth, I was an avid reader of science fiction. I was well-versed in the works of the Big Three. Clarke, Asimov and Heinlein. Isaac Asimov may have been the greatest science fiction writer of the three. He certainly was one of the greatest science fiction writers who was also a scientist. Most of the books he wrote are non-fiction books, not science fiction books.

The Big Three science fiction writers were a small group who created the core of the Golden Age of Science Fiction in the middle of the last century. Writers like Arthur C. Clarke, Robert Heinlein and L. Sprague de Camp. Oh yeah, even guys like L. Ron Hubbard was a part of this group of writers. Hubbard probably created the Church of Scientology on a "bet" made among these writers.

These guys inspired the 21st century. Much of the 21st century was shaped by these plot lines developed by these writers. Arguably, Isaac Asimov has been the most prophetic. His Three Laws of Robotics are a set of rules devised by the author. The rules were in his 1950 collection *I, Robot*.

The Three Laws are:

- *First Law- A robot may not injure a human being or, through inaction, allow a human being to come to harm.*
- *Second Law- A robot must obey the orders given it by human beings except where such orders would conflict with the First Law.*
- *Third Law- A robot must protect its own existence as long as such protection does not conflict with the First or Second Law.*

These laws form an organizing principle and unifying theme for Asimov's robotic-based fiction and the stories linked to it. These stories and these ideas have been a driving force toward the artificial intelligence we are now seeing.

Remember these ideas are from over SEVENTY years ago. Switch out artificial intelligence for the robots in his stories, and they become eerily prophetic. Asimov's visions still provide useful insight into our relationship with technology.

Frankly, most science fiction today is still rehashing the story lines spawned during this Golden Age of Science Fiction. It is the science fiction from the fifties which we still draw upon heavily despite the fact it is the 21st century. Asimov and his circle, outliers then, have become mainstream. Even in video games there are no new ideas. The often the story the game plays out against are just re-imagining of these writers' plot lines. However, these stories are very old despite the refreshment driven by media conversion.

Most science fiction these days revolves around technology, but good science fiction makes predictions about future societal evolution too. Predictions in science fiction now must include comic book superheroes. If they stray from the Marvel universe, then zombies or an apocalypse of some kind justifying special effects and action drive the narrative. These are not predictions of future societal evolution, but formula plat lines meant to make a profit.

Have we learned nothing new? Surely, in seventy years we have learned something and evolved somehow as a society. Have we not grown beyond them? Perhaps we have not. Why is our society socially stunted? Maybe we have been practicing social distancing for too long, and technology has had a hand in that?

Effective social distancing is a perfect example of where Asimov predicts societal evolution based upon technological advancements. COVID-19 brought it out as something technology could facilitate. Without technology, it cannot be considered. In his book, <u>The Naked Sun</u>, you see social distancing taken to an unexpected level. Back when I read the novel, it seemed impossible for any society to reach this level of disconnect from each other.

Even an "aspie" like me found it difficult to imagine a society like the socially distant one Asimov imagines. Yet, the pandemic has now put us firmly on this path.

COVID-19 has made this seem not so far-fetched any longer.

The aforementioned "anti-social" plot lines of Asimov's are from the I, Robot series of books. The robot series is one more people are familiar with due to Will Smith's movie of the same name. Asimov wrote other books, though. I submit to you they are equally as prophetic. I have begun to data-mine them to flesh out my inductively reasoned investment model.

Asimov's Foundation series of books are lesser-known but if they are as prophetic as the robot books, we are in for a rocky ride. In the Foundation series, again from seventy years ago, Asimov postulates a new science called psychohistory. The name is a misnomer because it is predictive analytics and chaos theory applied to humanity. In any case, psychohistory is the name Asimov gave it.

The story's primary psychohistorian is a man named Hari Seldon. The books are set in the future in which there is much strife and war in the galaxy. Through an application of math and artificial intelligence, Hari Seldon can make predictions about the future. He can put mankind back on the path to civil society and peace.

At least that is a driving plot point behind Asimov's series, the power for psychohistory to bring peace and prosperity to the galaxy. Psychohistory depends on the idea that, while one cannot foresee the actions of a particular individual, algorithms applied to large groups of people could predict the general flow of future events.

The character responsible for the science's creation, Hari Seldon, established two axioms:

1] *the population whose behavior was modeled should be sufficiently large*

2] *the population should remain in ignorance of the results of the application of psychohistorical analyses because if it is aware, the group changes its behavior.*

In the series of books, Hari Seldon does put humanity back on a stable footing. He creates a society heavily controlled by his psycho-historical predictions. These predictions were made years before and sealed only to be revealed at specific points in time. At each point, the power of psychohistory is driven home by the incredible accuracy of the predictions. Hari Seldon is remotely running society from the grave with these predictions made years and years before.

However, a random event finally throws the psychohistory predictions off-kilter. As Hari Seldon's predictive videos were released one by one, they also included advice for the current times the viewers were going through. Seldon knew ahead of time how things would be so he could give some advice. Things start to go astray as an unknown random event has thrown Seldon's predictions out of sync with the real events.

The pandemic has shown how a "random" event cannot be easily encoded into models or predicted by artificial intelligence. Unpredictable events of great consequence, make it very difficult for the investing-bots. The best investing AI algorithms rival Hari Seldon in their ability to make predictions about global behaviors

In the series Foundation, it is not a virus or a pandemic causing psychohistory's predictions to come off the rails. It turns to be a person. An unexpected person comes onto the scene. This person of unusual charisma changes the accuracy of the algorithm's predictions. In Asimov's Foundation stories, the random event is a person. This person is known as The Mule.

I submit to you that Isaac Asimov is our Hari Seldon. He has been predicting the future for us since just after World War II. His novels and stories defined a social future as it evolves in conjunction with technology. His books have made some surprising yet accurate predictions about 21st-century society.

Predictive analytics have been Asimov's great gift to us for over seventy years. His ideas provided a framework to understand our culture in the context of these new and powerful technologies. However, we are reaching the limits of Asimov's ability to predict the future. Donald Trump is our Mule for this timeline.

His actions have been very unexpected, starting with his election to the Presidency of the United States. His election is just one example of very unexpected events this century. Asimov tells us the Mule creates chaos. The Mule enjoys chaos. The Mule can operate effectively in chaos. The Mule changes the trajectory of society.

Ergo the future becomes far less predictable until a new trajectory is established. Big money players are beginning to wonder about the predictability of the future. This means less risky investing in some areas and more risky investing in other areas. The bets the AI systems are suggesting today are bit more risky.

I am pretty sure nobody, including AI, wants to bet money on the 2024 election right now. We all are effectively doing just that, though. Currently, everyone predicting reasonable stability in the US government transition of power in 2024.

How will we make decisions about where to put money between now and 2024? The older you are, the more important this decision becomes. Call it what you will, I like to think of it as the Time of the Mule. In any case, it may be science fiction modeling future events most accurately.

The GameStop drama illustrates the new world in investing. Hedge funds have taken losses in the billions by being targeted by an army of stimulus checks on Reddit. Derivatives are complicated algorithms making predictions about how money will move. We all know the most chaotic factor to calculate is human behavior.

Frankly, derivatives look a lot like what Asimov called psychohistory. Psychohistory depends on the idea that while one cannot foresee the actions of a particular individual, algorithms applied to large groups of people could predict the general flow of future events. Essentially, this is what derivative equations are doing for hedge funds.

Computers and algorithmic trading have been around for generations. Derivatives are simply complicated algorithms meant to guarantee returns over time. They along with the swaps used to bolster the guarantees came to the forefront of the financial conversation during the Great Recession. They continue to be a big deal with the recent Archegos fiasco.

Swaps are part of the derivative equation and help multiply the power of prediction through leverage. Bill Hwang, owner of Archegos, was able to take large positions with little collateral based upon his "family office" exemption and belief he had access to the best AI. He was able to do a "swap" deal with a bank where they were fronting him vast amounts of money. They believed the outcomes would be positive even though these were risky positions.

Big banks have been making money like this for generations now. Swaps are backroom deals between banks and big money. Big money has historically had access to the best computers and the best predictive analytics.

Coupled with inside track access, these seemingly risky bets have been SURE THING gambles that pay big. When you have insider info you can place big bets. When your predictive analytics are good, you can predict the behavior of investors. This makes profits a sure thing.

Banks are willing to make these secret swap deals with the very wealthy. Historically, these very rich people have had access to the best computers. They have had the best predictive analytics. That means if you front them money in these swap deals, their artificial intelligence guarantees massive profits. The banks make enormous amounts of money without taking much risk....unless there is a Black Swan event.

What if there are multiple Black Swan events? What if artificial intelligence is having problems making large scale predictions about the behavior of the masses. Increasingly irrational human behavior can play havoc with predictive analytics. The models used to build out these predictive analytics are too heavily based on old paradigms. The new paradigms have not been set.

Derivatives as complicated algorithms, make predictions about how money will move. These algorithms do need a framework of ideas and models to "score" the world and human behavior. We have finally outlived the grand visions of the great science fiction writers of the twentieth century. It is time for hedge funds to hire young science fiction writers to punch up their predictive analytics algorithms.

Psychohistory depends on the idea that while one cannot foresee the actions of a particular individual, algorithms applied to large groups of people can predict the general flow of future events. The derivative equations are making less accurate predictions. The population must be in relative ignorance for this model to work. They are no longer in ignorance. The results of the application of predictive analyses become less reliable when the population is aware, the group changes its behavior is being predicted. The pesky humans start to change.

Old science fiction has been predicting the future for us since just after World War II. They defined the future we now live in. Those ideas have certainly been a boon to the derivative industry. Hedge funds had the money to get the coders and leverage these ideas.

They had secret swap deals and the population remained in the dark about the manipulations. As we are roiled by crisis after crisis, the backroom deals are forced into the light. Their failures force transparency on how the money was lost. The **population is no longer ignorant.**

Less Analog Cash Means More Risk

Understanding physical money is paramount to understanding how currencies will evolve into the future. It is a simple concept. One must understand what came before to understand what comes next. However, it does seem likely physical money will be retired or heavily curtailed going forward. Despite record levels of liquidity physical cash is a shrinking portion of what has been historically been known as economy's "liquid" money, M1. No one argues this point any longer, analog money will eventually become an endangered species.

Currently, the world is awash in physical dollars. The US dollar is currency of the globe. All things are denominated in dollars. Being the world's reserve currency is very favorable for the United States. The logistics of keeping pallets of dollars in warehouses to do business has an enormous practical cost for the world though.

Compounding the logistical costs has been American foreign policy actions. The world's desire to retire the dollar as the global reserve currency is no longer even concealed any longer. Nations on every continent have questioned dollar hegemony.

Physical money will be retired. Its retirement brings great dangers to the dollar's position. Physical money represents the status quo. Physical money represents stability. Physical money represents a kind of transparency.

The fact a physical dollar bill exists in the world makes things less opaque. The transparency of physicality means it will be clear to the rest of the world when there are just too many dollars being created. Importantly, the rest of the world has been signaling its concern on this point for awhile now.

Nonetheless, as long as the world stays with physical money, the dollar's power is hard to beat. There are just so many in existence due to the long tenure as the world's reserve currency. Even as the United States has turned up the regulations and sanctions around using the dollar, it remains an indispensable instrument of doing business globally. Even rival countries have dollars on hand for this very reason. One can imagine how this grates them a bit.

The world's reserve currency is a physical dollar, but the move away from physical currencies is accelerating. There are transfers of wealth happening all the time without any physical currency being exchanged. All this wealth is currently denominated in dollars. This is the reality of today, a digital general ledger representing the physical system.

There are digital versions of the dollar in accounting systems worldwide. These are not cryptocurrencies and are still bound to this old system. A system tied to a physical global reserve currency called the US dollar. The 21st-century sovereign currencies are simply computerized versions of old-style fiat. This is all controlled by the nation-states and the bankers.

Already some countries are nearly free of physical money with most transactions being done digitally. However, these are not public blockchains. If they were, they could provide transparency to money movements. We are in a dangerous moment of transition. A true 21st-century monetary system is evolving beyond a digital representation of the 20th-century one.

In New Zealand, there is only enough physical money to cover about 5% of the money in citizen accounts. If 6% of New Zealand citizens withdraw their money due to some panic, the system would be in crisis and perhaps even collapse. There is an extreme disconnect in New Zealand between the assets stored digitally as savings and the actual physical currency available.

New Zealand's size may make this an acceptable and stable situation. The island nation can reach out to global resources if such a panic did occur. Economies the size of the United States are a different story. All of the digital assets can change in value quickly. A fatal contagion spreading through the United States can take down the global system faster than ever before.

I am old enough to have had grandparents who lived through the Great Depression. Their childhood stories to me were filled with images of extreme poverty. It made me very interested in the Depression. When I read history books, I sought precursor signs in the events that led up to it. My grandparents' stories were enough to make me desperate to avoid ever experiencing it in person.

My grandparents had lots of stories. They intimated how rumors could create problems. If gossip began to circulate of bank insolvency, a run on assets at the banks was a foregone conclusion. When it happened, you better have some cash on hand at home. Otherwise, it was barter for this or that until the banks opened again…IF they opened again.

Despite the thirties being an era with a much lesser disconnect between the amount depositors had stored on the ledger versus the physical supply, there were still issues. A run on the banks in the United States threatened the global financial system. Already by the 1930s the size of the American economy made its health affect the world's health.

The repeated runs on the banks led FDR to close the banks for days. He recognized that he needed to stop the bleeding. It was a breather, so the system could get resources in place. Such are the limitations of an analog system that physical resources can take time to marshal.

One could be forgiven for seeing today's digital improvements as far superior. After all, these resources can be brought to bear so much quicker and easier. In 2008, when the credit market froze causing a global crisis many resources pushed into the system quickly. The Great Recession brought on by credit default swaps has faded from memory. It was a relatively short term event compared to the Great Depression.

Little regulation has been applied since the Great Recession of 2008-09 to prevent similar risky behavior by financial institutions. The event was so short-lived compared to the Great Depression. The short-lived nature made the system seem more resilient. After all, banks did not have to close during the Great Recession. However, we learned later that things were right on the brink in 2008. We still do not fully understand how bad things were in 2008, I believe.

Ironically in the Information Age, information is more controlled than ever before. The digital revolution now allows for more control of the distribution of information rather than facilitating a wide distribution of useful knowledge. It is not widely known or discussed, but this the run on the banks during the Great Recession was significant.

Wealth was fleeing the American financial institutions very quickly in the summer of 2008. The flight of "cash" nearly crashed the financial system. The reasons to move back to Glass-Steagall and other regulations born from the Great Depression seem quite justified, but it has not been done.

Instead, there is a widespread feeling 2008 was not really that bad. Apparently, the freezing up of global credit is not really a crash. To modern monetary theorists 2008 was just a fender bender. The solution is always create more cash.

We should know better. The Great Recession was a Great Warning in my opinion. A warning Americans did not heed. Had there been a more physical system of money in place, Americans would have been a lot more frightened in 2008. There would have been empty ATMs and long lines to get limited amounts of cash.

We now know there were huge outflows of digital cash from American financial instruments in the Great Recession. There was so much pressure on US financial institutions that money market funds in 2008 began to break below a dollar. This was significant because money markets were seen as savings accounts back then.

Money market funds are NOT digital cash, they are financial instruments with shares that can trade for any number. These mutual funds had been designed to be pegged to the dollar in such a way that each share was worth a dollar. The Great Recession pulled the rug out from under everyone. These shares were trading for less than a dollar in the Summer of 2008.

Money market funds were acting as a rival reserve currency which was essentially digital. Shares in dollar denominated money markets were signaling a different value for the world's reserve currency. The United States had lost control of the value of its currency.

There was not a lot of obvious evidence of the financial crisis by the Fall of 2008. There was a lot of breathless Congressional testimony. Some of it sounded almost hysterical to Main Street. Everything seemed fine, but Americans were being told a trillion dollars were necessary to "save the system".

It was not until later in 2009, the average person started to see the effects of what had happened the previous summer. The stealthy nature of financial instability with computers moving money so quickly is being ignored. There is not much to do about it. One can engage in a small campaign of civil disobedience and use cash at every turn, but in the 3=21st century too few people see the utility of this.

In the late 20th century, there was another financial crisis caused by poorly regulated investment instruments. Junk bonds and the savings and loan crisis roiled American financial systems in the late eighties. Surprisingly, I learned there might be problems in the system before it was nationwide news.

On the way to work, I saw a line outside of Tahoe Savings and Loan in Rancho Cordova, CA. There was a physical manifestation to the savings and loan crisis. Before it really started showing itself in the financial markets broadly, there were some physical manifestations.

In 2008, no such physical manifestation of a possible run on our banks presented itself. Obviously, Congress was given access to the financial information or they would not have been a trillion dollars of taxpayer money sent off to make foreign investors whole. The United States government backstopped everything to prevent a complete collapse of the global financial systems. They understood the consequences of the failure of the dollar-based system.

Smart people the world round recognized how close the American economy had been to dragging everyone into a global depression. The lack of transparency in computerized financial systems was recognized as a huge risk. With less and less physical cash as a real world pulse on the health of the system, there was more danger. It meant computerized "shenanigans" could obfuscate issues until it was too late.

Banks are supposed to be stodgy stewards of the financial systems. As some of the biggest stakeholders in financial assets, bankers act as "proof of stake" validators in our current financial system. In 2008, it became clear they were no longer reliable. A new digital "proof of work" concept was needed and Bitcoin was born from the Great Recession of 2008-09

Banks No Longer Have a Value Proposition

Bitcoin and cryptocurrencies are born against the backdrop of financial chaos in 2008-09. The central bankers had not provided the regulatory oversight expected. Despite the fact these bankers were some of the biggest stakeholders in the financial systems, they allowed it to be corrupted. When the world went off the gold standard, the biggest stakeholders in the system were entrusted with regulating it.

The "proof of stake" idea is not a new one. The idea is the biggest stakeholders make the biggest profits when the system is trusted and used. It in their interest in providing a fair and stable capital market. The world would do business in the markets which seemed most governed by the rule of law and most fair. The largest stakeholders had the most to gain if the world perceived the United States as the global bankers.

The gold standard is a sort of "proof of work" system, because it is hard to get gold. It takes a lot of work to get gold. Possessing gold generally meant some "work" had been done to obtain it. In 2008, it became clear the fiat system's "proof of stake" processes were not working. The biggest stakeholders made the biggest profits when they allowed the system to be corrupted.

This can only go on for a finite time until the infidelity of the stakeholders is exposed and some new system put in place. The digital age required a new "proof of work" commodity was the most important lesson of the Great Recession. This is how Bitcoin was born and why it is often referred to as digital gold. The 2008-09 financial crisis birthed the cryptocurrency revolution.

There is a lot more to be written about 2008. There were rumors the US had been involved in the dust-up in South Ossetia. South Ossetia was part of Georgia on the southern Russian border. In 2008, the Russians were flush with cash.

Could the Russians have attacked the American financial markets in retaliation for our meddling? If one looks back at the events leading up to the crisis, there are some "trends". Certainly, 2008 signaled heightened tensions between Russia and the United States.

Russia's financial might is pint-sized in comparison to the Chinese economy. The rivalry between China and the United States is likely to roil financial markets more, not less. To imagine this rivalry will not extend into currency markets is naive. The need for some "extra-national" currency is becoming more and more obvious. Cryptocurrencies have plenty of utility in this multi-polar world of competing interests.

Banks have no real value proposition any longer when they are paying no interest to depositors. Banks have held on as a "facilitator", even enforcer of financial norms. They are still seen as a necessary evil. However, fewer and fewer hold the belief that banks are a necessary evil. They are corrupt and simply evil is becoming the new perception of banks.

There has been much consternation about the possibility of negative interest rates. The Federal Reserve has gone out of its way to calm the fears of bankers and other financial titans. Those are inspirational words but for most people interest rates have been negative for some time.

For most of the 21st century, the poorer you were the more you were experiencing negative interest rates. The amount of fees the banking industry has been allowed to extract from its clientele without providing ANY value effectively calculates out to negative interest rates unless one has very large balances. Since 2008, the Federal Reserve has been paying banks better interest than the banks have been paying depositors.

American banks are no longer filling their traditional role. They are engaged in predatory practices which are destructive to the economy. They offer no premium for allowing them access to depositor money. They feel entitled to put in on the wheel in the Wall Street casinos. Once they offered a premium for holding depositor money.

Additionally, banks promised not to engage in risky investments, but were conservative stewards of the capital. Banks were entrusted with the fuel for business. They once invested in the middle class. Banks supported long term wealth accumulation through a stable economy.

Their predatory practices have become intolerable. To anyone with REAL money, banks are nearly useless. The convenience factor is significantly reduced when the banks charge such a premium for the convenience. Real money has many other places to store wealth. Poorer Americans have to pay for the convenience of banks as it remains a real thing for poorer citizens.

Americans are not all stupid though. They are searching for alternatives. Many younger people believe they may not really need a bank in the future. Cryptocurrencies could fill this role as well. Regardless of the party in power, government seems to be most closely allied with the bankers not the citizenry. Younger citizens are seeking alternatives to a closed system and this may hasten the demise of banks.

US Markets No Longer Offer Price Discovery

The soaring stock market during the pandemic has been a bit troubling. The stock market is supposed to be a measure of economic activity, not divergence. However, the Federal Reserve has been stimulating the economy for over a decade now. The excuse has been hitting an arbitrary 2 percent inflation target.

To their credit, the Federal Reserve did try to clear the balance sheets in 2017 and 2018. As they allowed bond purchases to expire, they also hiked interest rates. These were the right actions to take though I would say they were a bit late in the cycle and should have been applied a couple of years earlier.

Naturally, this caused the stock market to come down a bit. As safer investments appear capitalist theory says money should move there. When that money moves out of the market, the laws of supply and demand say stock prices should go down. These are basic macro factors when investing in free markets.

Within the broader economic cycle, there are changes within sectors and within individual companies. Once upon a time, reviewing accounting reports, public filings and economic charts could provide information for the American investor. Within macroeconomic cycles, transparent accounting practices means investors can make informed decisions. Quarterly reporting in free markets allows investors to make adjustments to their investments based upon open accounting. This creates "price discovery".

"Price discovery" is the great attraction of the American markets. The rule of law and transparent accounting have combined to create an environment in the USA where investors can have confidence. Foreign and domestic investors alike prefer facts which are real and validated. This situation is no longer quite as obvious in the American markets. There will be consequences as foreign investor distrust grows.

In 2018, the political cost of doing the right thing and allowing the stock market to pull back while reducing the Federal Reserve's involvement was deemed too expensive. A foreign investor expecting price discovery to still be valid got burned. The view was the stock market would pull back. Many dumped out before the downturn of late 2018 because in well-regulated markets, the cycles are "managed" but not suppressed.

Many investors were well-positioned to make money awaiting the small and healthy downturn. Shockingly, the Federal Reserve, under pressure from the White House, began supporting the market and economy as if there was a recession going on.

These "smart" positions became very unprofitable. Foreign investors may have felt robbed. Cutting interest rates during economic expansion traditionally causes asset inflation. It has pumped up the stock market. It also means those who have invested based upon normal economic factors can lose a lot of money when natural market cycles are suppressed.

Foreign investor bears found the Federal Reserve's action throughout 2019 to be a bit annoying. **The amount of money printing which followed means the American economy is flush with cash. There is cash to be invested but few places paying anything like a reasonable return.**

The central government and the central bank have dropped trillions of cash into the economy. There is great demand for securities but good information is sparse. It makes many stock purchases feel like gambling. Worse, Fed officials appear to have made investments ahead of market moving decisions at the central bank.

Foreign and domestic investors alike would surely like to know ahead of time what stocks might the Federal Reserve be buying. One wonders what corporate bonds are they buying? Apple has issued forty-year corporate debt and there is interest. Will the US government be buying these bonds? Do politicians making decisions about such things own stock in the same companies the government buys?

The involvement of the central government and central bank in the markets has killed any price discovery credibility which remained. Without any transparency on who gains when certain assets are purchased by the central government, the stench of corruption is everywhere. In this new corrupt environment, the tax returns of politicians are now optional.

In an environment like this, how can price discovery exist? The price of an asset must be determined by the free market for price discovery to exist. For hard work to pay off, credible information must be available. Transparent knowledge about the assets of those who pull the levers of the money printing presses is an absolute requirement. How does one invest in an environment where this information is not available?

Is Tim Cooke Starting a Rollerball League

Undoubtedly 2020 brought a great deal of upheaval and change. It exposed many flaws in the current state of affairs. Change is everywhere. Corruption is everywhere as well though.

Investing has become more uncertain. I feel lucky to have grown up on the stories of the great science fiction writers of the twentieth century. Writers like Asimov and Heinlein have been prophetic.

Early immersion in these forward-thinking plot lines made 2020 a bit easier to cope with. It also made me sensitive to trends which follow other old plot lines. I have already pointed out plot lines from the mid 20th century which have begun to be germane today, like Asimov's Foundation series.

There was a rich assortment of plot lines supplied by many talented writers back then. Some predicted the decline of nation-states with the power vacuum filled by corporations. We are on the verge of corporate nation states today. Some would argue they are already extant.

There are trillion dollar corporations now. Wal-Mart and the Walton family have more financial power than half the nations in the United Nations. There are many multi-billionaires on the planet today. Jeff Bezos has more money than Iceland or Azerbaijan!

Azerbaijan has enough money to make war though. They regularly clash with Armenia. These "little wars" cost money. Nothing demonstrates the obsolescence of nation-states like the foolishness of war.

I make no political comment here nor push any ideology. It is an undeniable fact the United Nations is a failed organization. This failure makes wars, big and small, more likely. The retail investor must deal in hard facts. War is one of those pesky facts, unfortunately.

War is usually about borders which are often about control of economic resources. Historically nation-states of diverse populations have been held together by shared economic interests. Their shared interests mean they invest in a shared military to defend the borders. Of course, many nations are all about ethnicity and cultural heritage, but not all. The United States demonstrated the power of a diverse population with shared economic interests.

The 21st century is defining new norms every day. The pandemic has accelerated this, but it was always happening. The pandemic has also demonstrated responsible governance matters when there is so much change. This is the greatest gift of the nation state, a peaceful and stable environment within which a company can do business.

An environment of chaos is not suitable for business. An environment without a stable social foundation will not last. Many a corporation and nation-state has collapsed due to cultural issues rather than bad business models. In so many ways, the multi-national corporation is another type of nation-state.

Responsible governance and good leadership in the nation-states is becoming scarce. When leadership cannot get along, there is no true guidance coming from the top. Responsible governance can provide continuity of leadership, and the rule of law.

The 21st century is changing how a stable environment can be provided for citizens. Technology is making the virtual world as important as the physical world. Enormous power in the virtual world can translate to power in the physical world. Apple may have reached the critical mass necessary to define a virtual nation state.

Apple has achieved this critical mass as the first trillion dollar company. Tim Cook seems to understand what it means. Apple has a lot of power. It needs to exert that power to preserve it, especially when there is so much change happening.

Apple leadership was put in a bind by the trade war with China. Tim Cook and his board have been forced to deal with a chaotic economic environment. Apple may have the ability to provide economic stability. Corporations need stability just like retail investors.

Apple appears to be large enough to create a stable environment for itself and others. Apple already has a group of very passionate "citizens". Many people will ONLY use Apple products. Apple also works very hard to preserve a virtual walled garden. This keeps their user base in all things Apple.

Apple is one of the two big mobile operating system providers. Along with Google, Apple processes every text message not as a public utility but as a private corporation. Texting is vital infrastructure. Yet, it is the corporations which provide it.

On top of the infrastructure services, Apple has near unbreakable encryption. Apple famously thumbed its nose at the FBI several years ago when they were asked to unlock an iPhone. The US government went to an Israeli tech firm to get the phone unlocked.

Tim Cook has at his disposal the resources of a trillion-dollar corporation. He has millions of passionate citizens. Recent events have been signaling the possibility of civil unrest and more instability in the country. While we have been struggling with these issues, Tim Cook has been putting the pieces in place to help Apple continue to operate anticipating a failure on this front.

During the summer of 2020 **Apple issued 40-year bonds**. At the time, these bonds were paying twice the US 30-year bond. **Apple corporate bonds** were snatched up quickly. Apple received a trillion dollars to do with it as it would. All Apple has to do is pay the sub 3% interest rate on these bonds annually.

At the time, many wondered why Apple needed the money. Most commented the company was simply taking advantage of shrinking interest rates from sovereign nations. In late 2018, Apple started working with the XRP parent Ripple. In 2019, Apple had integrated Ripple's Interledger into Apple Pay.

In 2020, speculation started to become broader. Was Apple going to use this huge haul from the bonds to absorb Ripple and the cryptocurrency XRP? Could be absorbing Ripple so the Apple Corporate State will have a national currency?

Laughing? No one can say 2020 showed the United States as a place of social or economic stability. Sure the stock market soared, but the rest of the country became divided against itself. There is social unrest everywhere. The rule of law is no longer a given.

Apple has the money, the citizenry, the encryption, the currency to create a virtual nation state. All they need to create a stable economic environment is the will to create one. I started really believing Apple and Tim Cook were not going to sit back and allow their grand economic paradise of Apple World to be destroyed by a ridiculous and counterproductive trade war.

Once the economic stability is provided, others will look to the Apple model. If nation-states cannot provide economic stability for citizens, then they will look for "authorities" that can do so. Corporate nation-states may just become a necessity if nationalism continues to hurt business and threaten global stability.

My speculation was based upon a science fiction movie of the seventies titled Rollerball. If you have not seen what the Rollerball world looks like, **Turner Classic Movies periodically trots out the 1975 movie** starring James Caan and John Houseman. It is a decent movie.

It is also far more prophetic than I would ever have believed when I saw it all those years ago. It foretells a dystopian tale. It is a tough future. The retail investor will need to be nimble and adapt in a Rollerball environment.

I bought some Ripple about this time as "bet" on this plot line.

SEC Objects to Rollerball League

It seemed as if **Apple was beginning to sketch out the boundaries of a virtual corporate state**. I felt good about using the Rollerball plot line to model reality. It seemed we were headed for a world where corporate states were the big dogs. Apple's moves in the Ripple universe were hard to ignore in this context so I threw some money at Ripple in the Fall of 2020.

However, it was naive to think such things would go unnoticed by the United States government. American power is now almost solely based upon the fact the dollar is the world's reserve currency. Over 50% of transactions in the world are denominated in the dollar. When the United States government puts sanctions on companies or individuals, they have real bite.

It can be very difficult for individuals to transact business in the 21st century. American sanctions against countries cause real pain in this environment. It is why the **Iranians are working so hard in the cryptocurrency universe**. Tehran has quite a hash rate in the Bitcoin universe. They need to get around these sanctions. The dollar hegemony is the ultimate power on the globe and has been for some time. The United States government completely understands this.

The fiasco known as the Search for WMD in Iraq may have been about this currency power the United States wields. Most of the world's transactions have been about oil over the decades. Oil is denominated in dollars of course. The petrodollar monopoly means all nations need to have large amounts of dollars stockpiled.

As the 20th century ended, Iraq began a Euro-denominated oil market. The threat to the **petrodollar monopoly may have been the real reason behind the catastrophic invasion** of Iraq. The search for Weapons of Mass Destruction took center stage. The direct attack on a Euro-denominated petroleum market received almost no coverage at the time. The inductive reasoner may feel it makes sense in retrospect.

Given the understanding by United States leadership of the incredible power of being the reserve currency, I feel very foolish in retrospect. I believed Apple and Ripple we going to be allowed to move forward with their plans unimpeded.

Bitcoin started to really take off in 2020. Ripple did as well. XRP was about to break seventy cents. I felt like an investing genius. In reality, it was unlikely the US could ignore Apple's moves on this front. The Ripple party was halted by the news of the lawsuit.

The United States trained its regulatory powers upon a possible "corporate currency". Despite other countries, like the Japanese, the United States government ruled Ripple was a security. Given **the Japanese and others have already ruled on this matter,** the United States seems late to the game making this ruling. Despite being late, the United States sees the fact a corporate state with its own currency as threat. It may be a greater threat to dollar hegemony than any other developments.

Let us be clear I lost money on this deal. The ruling by the SEC had a serious affect on the price of XRP. Anyone who bought Ripple in the summer of 2020 was sorry by Halloween. The inductive reasoning investor in the United States has limited access to RELIABLE information. That is why they are leveraging their inductive reasoning powers in the first place.

Following this science fiction plot line had cost me money. Nonetheless, I hold onto my XRP knowing Apple has staying power in the courtroom and they have some interest here. However, this is not exactly a known outcome. Apple could lose interest, learn from its mistake and pick a different cryptocurrency to move forward with. Read no further if you could not stomach such an unexpected and somewhat unfair loss. It should serve as a warning to other cryptocurrency investors in other coins, including Bitcoin. The United States regulatory power can become a real threat to wealth.

The government has yet to make a serious attempt to regulate cryptocurrency. When it does, there will be winners and losers, but it will be hard to tell ahead of time. Additionally, the level of corruption in government means some will know ahead of time.

Losses will be staggering if one is on the wrong side of the regulation. This is why I made sure to write at the beginning about owning one's decisions. We are making educated guesses at best in the cryptocurrency universe.

Jack Ma's Rollerball Team

Despite losing money on the XRP debacle, the Rollerball plot line held my attention. It got more support as 2020 evolved. Apple was beginning to sketch out the boundaries of a virtual corporate state, and there were others with similar dreams. There are so many large corporate entities in this world.

China hosts a lot of these corporate giants. Alibaba Group, owned by Jack Ma, is the Amazon of Asia. This makes Jack Ma the Chinese Jeff Bezos. Alibaba created a service called Alipay, a system for making payments by phone, using QR codes. It's now used for billions of transactions and is making cash nearly obsolete in China.

Jack Ma's companies handles half of all the transactions being done in China! Jack Ma is a very powerful billionaire in China. If Jack Ma decided to use a particular cryptocurrency or come up with one of his own, it would compete directly with China's Central Bank cryptocurrency, the digital renminbi.

China is ahead of the United States on the cryptocurrency front. China has its a digital currency already. It has seeded it into the economy through large airdrops, essentially giving their digital currency away. The Chinese are very much the leaders with a digital sovereign currency.

Jack Ma's Alipay was spun off into a company called Ant Financial. Last fall, Ant Financial was heading for an initial public offering of stock, potentially the largest IPO in history. Suddenly, Chinese regulators suspended the IPO.

Then Jack Ma went missing! He has not been seen in public for quite a long time. I hope for his sake the rumors are true and he has simply been told to lay low. However, some sources are reporting, **'He is embracing supervision at an undisclosed location.'** The Chinese government has been quite aggressive in asserting control of its territories, real AND VIRTUAL.

The Chinese recognize the power of a currency. The United States has been able to get away with a lot of deficit spending because the dollar is the reserve currency. In the 20th century, physical money was still a thing. Governments all around the world have stockpiled dollars on pallets to do business.

This physical supply of dollars is high bar to entry for a competing reserve currency. It can take a long time to create enough physical currency for a reserve challenger to even exist. A digital currency could be a quick way to achieve reserve currency status, because it can exist in the virtual world only. If your currency was seen as secure compared to other digital currencies adoption could be swift. It is all about trust and utility. If your currency offered superior 21st century capabilities, like smart contracts, adoption would be an easy decision.

There will be no physical limitation to the quickness it is stockpiled or moved about. A digital currency can be deployed as a new reserve currency, if the world decides to go there. There will be treaties. A new financial age will be haled. America's special pedestal in the global monetary system will evaporate.

China is taking firm control of money in all its forms behind the Great Firewall. My Ripple investment may have been on the wrong side of the battle between the nation states and nascent corporate states, but it confirmed the Rollerball hypothesis. China's actions against Jack Ma further ensure its validity.

What of the dollar? Perhaps the aforementioned digital reserve currency will be a binary sawbuck? I am unsure. If we get one, I might buy some.

As for Jack Ma, I wish him well. I have a feeling "embracing supervision" is not very fun. It sounds like "enhanced interrogation", but I am sure it is just a translation problem.

Who Else Might Have Rollerball Plans

The Ripple bet may have gone south, but the idea of corporate states becoming a thing got more support. Jack Ma's problems surfaced and his IPO blocked by Beijing, because the Chinese Communist Party recognized the threat of rogue billionaires. The blocking of the Ant IPO was confirmation the nation-state versus corporate-state battle was happening. It further confirmed at least one nation-state had realized the threat cryptocurrency could have to the power of the nation-states. I started looking around for who else might be interested in starting a Rollerball team. LOL

Elon Musk is one of the richest people on the planet. Elon is planning to expand his footprint in the Solar System. Elon has been talking up an aggressive timeline for putting a human on Mars. Once he gets there, Elon promises to break ground on a Mars colony almost immediately. The timeline he puts forth is ridiculously aggressive. If he gets there at all, it will be an amazing accomplishment.

Elon has also said this colony would most likely transact business in a cryptocurrency. Elon is a billionaire, so he knows any colony will have an economy. The capitalist nature of humans simply demands it. Otherwise you go, come back, and just rest on your laurels as the United States did after Apollo.

To have a state one must have a currency. It is why "sovereign" can reference a monarchy, a nation OR a currency. Elon's off-world holdings could become policed by his corporate proxies. That Elon Musk may have sovereign ambitions became a real idea for me.

Nation-states can be quite protective of their power though. The SEC has sued Ripple claiming the company's cryptocurrency XRP is a security not a currency. Another very powerful player in the future of money, Jack Ma disappeared. One cannot blame Elon for being a little coy here. His irreverence is a smokescreen. I began to pay a lot more attention.

Elon Musk cannot deny his interest in cryptocurrencies, especially Dogecoin. He even had his Twitter profile read "former CEO of Dogecoin". He has since removed it. Nonetheless, he had become quite an icon in the Dogecoin community after his 2019 election as pseudo-CEO.

Things got hot and heavy in December of 2020 though. Elon was tweeting about Dogecoin a lot. On Christmas, the infamous sexy boxers tweet sent things skyrocketing in the Dogecoin universe. I started to really take notice here.

I started thinking a lot about the fact Elon had all of this tech at SpaceX. Tesla had access to that tech so I had invested, I realized it gave Elon more leverage than Jack Ma. The rise of the corporate state seems inevitable. now. Elon knows he needs a currency and seems to like dogecoin.

I jumped in and bought some. When my friends needled me a bit, I ended up convincing myself to buy more. I have convinced myself Elon is going to do something with Dogecoin.

I have even convinced myself it does not really matter whether Elon does something with Dogecoin. It really does have a value proposition and another nation, could pick it up. As an existing ecosystem, it makes sense due to it's great supply. I believe someone or something is going to leverage the billions of Doge.

Still, I think Elon simply does not want to overplay his hand. Elon is patient. Everything is pointing in his favor. Why end up hamstrung like Apple and Ripple? He has already had to deal with a lot of SEC attention. It is probably no fun. And Jack Ma's "embrace of supervision" seems very unfun.

We cannot blame Elon for backing away. Of course, he must. When asked about Dogecoin, he is coy. Musk may have the clearest path to a Rollerball team as any billionaire or corporation on the planet.

In my opinion, Elon Musk is the most likely candidate. He has his personal and corporate wealth for creating some "independent entity" outside of nation-state power. I started to imagine it. He could start with a low orbit space station. It is private. It will be the SpaceX police patrolling the halls.

The Rollerball Cryptocurrency Hypothesis was born. All the science fiction I had read as a child finally seemed worth it. I felt real certainty this hypothesis had some value. I kept scolding myself for not putting my money where my mouth was…or where my ideas were.

I knew it was an unusual idea. Those that come up with new ideas have to have confidence in themselves. They have to put their own money into it at first.

The Rollerball Cryptocurrency Hypothesis

By the end of 2020, I had fully bought into the Rollerball Cryptocurrency Hypothesis. It felt weird to be thinking about moving money based upon old science fiction plot lines, but by the end of 2020 nothing seemed weird any longer. Anything seemed possible now.

My mind had already been speculating along the lines of Isaac Asimov and his Foundation series and the idea of Donald Trump representing the Mule character. His election and actions as president were so far outside previous norms, and he broke a number of predictive models. It is hard to argue this man did not create new norms no matter one's politics.

As a longtime coder, I understood Apple and Google controlled the text messaging universe. SMS for all its flaws is still a base communication protocol in the United States and the world. In the US, many cities use SMS for their emergency alert systems. However, the two mobile phone operating systems maintain a sort of monopoly on cross platform delivery. They do such a fine job no one complains.

The pandemic brought enormous pressures upon governments at all levels in the United States. The idea to protect one another from each other's viral cloud by wearing a face mask became a flash point. In California, one local health official lamented that people simply did not want to be governed any longer. Face mask mandates and lockdowns came at the corporate and state levels in the United States. National government was demonstrably broken.

Once vaccines became available, it became a struggle to get some to take the jab. Again corporations are leading the way by mandating vaccinations for employees to return to work. Visas and travel papers noting vaccination status are nothing new to travelers, but COVID-19 politicized it in the United States.

Nonetheless, the practical need for such vaccine "passports" is undeniable. Common sense capitalism dictates an easy way to verify whether someone has been vaccinated against a virus which shut down economic activity in 2020. Most likely, mobile phones will become the repositories of this vital information. Corporations will need this information easily available and Apple and Google will make it easy to do in Android and iOS.

If nation states cannot provide economic stability for citizens and the corporations that employ them, then they will look for "authorities" that can facilitate this stability. Corporate nation-states may become a necessity. Nationalism continues to hurt business in the United States and threaten global stability.

Against this backdrop, the idea of corporate nation-states as portrayed in the movie Rollerball seemed more likely than ever before in my lifetime. I really loved this old science fiction movie of the seventies titled Rollerball. I enjoyed John Houseman portrayal of corporate power in a future world dominated by corporations not nation states.

Rollerball feels far more prophetic than I would ever have believed when I saw it all those years ago. It foretells a dystopian tale for the United States. If this is the future, it is a tough future. Being a capitalist, I started to wonder what this meant to me as a retail investor. Clearly, I would need to be nimble and adapt.

My precious metals and short positions started to look fantastic in March 2020. I held them, but then the great stimulus spewed money all over the economy. Price discovery began to disappear.

It became very hard to figure out what would happen next. The government was acting as a price insensitive buyer of so many different things in the economy. My short positions went back to being money losers.

This idea that big corporations were going to be the winners became abundantly clear. Tesla had government contracts at the highest levels such that when he smoked a doobie there was a meltdown at the Pentagon. I figured he knew more than he was letting on. Inductive reasoning meant Tesla would benefit by being first to market with technologies which are currently unknown. I threw money into the Tesla bucket.

As the summer of 2020 progressed, I continued to believe the billionaires were not going to lose. I decided to throw a lot of money at Amazon. This turned out to be a lot less lucrative than Tesla. We were late to that party.

Everyone understood the billionaires were not going to lose. Investors jumping into the billionaire's boats. It was a crowded trade. How to get ahead of that idea?

Finally, Tim Cook showed some cards. Apple issued forty-year bonds. The bonds were sucked up. When I learned of Apple's involvement with Ripple, the idea for the *Rollerball Cryptocurrency Hypothesis* hit me. It just sounded cool even if I was not going to put money on it...or was I?

Next thing I knew I found myself buying a bunch of Ripple. Initially this looked like it might have been a successful implementation of the Rollerball Cryptocurrency Hypothesis. However, the SEC attacked Ripple. Nonetheless, it helped confirm the hypothesis might be true. I decided I needed a bit more Ripple. I figured Apple/Ripple would pay some fines and move forward with their Rollerball League.

Now I was putting new money into cryptocurrency based upon the belief there would be a Rollerball League. What I mean by a Rollerball League is corporate city-states. I was putting money into the idea that cryptocurrency will be the basis of new private corporate economies.

These ecosystems will continue to rise. They will be embraced by people looking for economic stability. These corporate city-states will be the ones who can provide economic stability. Or at least that is what I reckoned with my Ripple stash.

Things did not go exactly as planned though as the Chinese leadership started making moves. They clearly believed the Rollerball world was imminent. Xi and the CCP decided self-sufficient corporate economies needed to be curtailed. Poor Jack Ma is still "embracing supervision" at this writing.

The SEC and the Chinese are now acting like corporate economies using cryptocurrencies are a real threat to nation-state power. This confirms the Rollerball Cryptocurrency Hypothesis validity. The nation-states are putting obstacles in the path of a small investor trying to maintain wealth in the new world.

A titanic struggle between nation-states and corporate entities is now extant. Nation-states will use their power to make law to fight back. I had learned the hard way the path to cryptocurrency adoption was fraught with regulatory dangers.

When the SEC filed suit against Ripple, XRP's price dropped significantly. Nation-states now understood. They would attempt to control these new forms of money. Corporate states would seek to retain their growing independence. The small investor would be caught in the middle. This was one conclusion to be definitively drawn from events.

In light of this struggle, capitalizing on the Rollerball Cryptocurrency Hypothesis looked like it might be difficult. When, **Elon Musk** started tweeting about Dogecoin in late 2020, I took notice.

I thought, "Wow, there is a billionaire paying attention to Dogecoin."

I start thinking maybe I need to get some Dogecoin in late 2020. I buy a little before the end of the year, but I am not feeling smart. I feel like I am investing based upon a billionaire's tweets. It feels dumb.

However, I am comforted by one fact. I have an operating model I am using to follow a strategy. I am not some fanboy following Dogefather Elon's tweets. I follow his tweets because he checks a lot of boxes in the Rollerball Cryptocurrency Hypothesis.

Cryptocurrencies will be adopted by the coming corporate pseudo-states. Elon Musk is the boldest billionaire. He will be first. At least that is what I keep telling myself.

Frankly, the 2020 election did not leave me with a warm and fuzzy feeling about my country. Whether I love the United States or not is no longer the point. There no longer appears to be a truly functional country. As 2021 dawns, the country seems to be running on inertia.

There is more and more debate about the election in December of 2020. There is real doubt about whether the election will be certified. These are facts. Facts are the foundation of any retail investing strategy in such uncertain times.

In an era of Fake News, facts seem quite hard to come by. I am a bit disheartened by the chaos in the central government. Finally, the Rollerball Cryptocurrency Hypothesis leads me to officially "follow" Elon on Twitter.

Some time in December of 2020, I stopped just lurking on his feed and just clicked follow. He keeps tweeting about Dogecoin. In the first week of 2021, Dogecoin is a theme for him.

By now, I had convinced myself Elon would be the first billionaire to pull off an autonomous corporate state. Starbase in Texas had filed for incorporation. There seems little doubt this will be a corporate city. I imagine Dogecoin as the only currency inside the city limits.

At t hat point, I reluctantly sliced off a piece of a Bitcoin. I felt I had to act on my hypothesis. I bought a chunk of Dogecoin. I made the decision based upon the <u>Rollerball Cryptocurrency Hypothesis</u>.

Yes, I did do exactly this. I made my investing decisions based upon old science fiction plot lines. Now I have written a book about how I am modeling a very nebulous future.

I believe the near past does not inform the near future. Most of the time it does, but during times of great change it is a mirage. The future will be significantly different from here. Nobody knows what exactly the future holds, including me.

Some amount of cryptocurrency allows one to be a little more agile, if the future becomes even more unexpected. I am old and retirement is looming. I simply cannot afford to be on the wrong side of a big change. I feel it is better to put some money on the wheel as a hedge against unexpected events.

Little did I know how unexpected things were going to become. The dawn of 2021 saw some very unexpected events. I was very surprised by them, but I knew I could not ignore them. Certain things cannot be ignored. When problems present themselves, especially BIG problems, the first thing people want to do is deny there is such a big problem. The first step to dealing with big problems is recognizing they exist. The next step is avoiding a blamestorm, because truly big problems will not be solved by such wasted time.

Jeff Bezos Saves the Republic

In January 2021, following Elon Musk was looking lucrative. Picking up a little bit of Dogecoin at the beginning of the year seemed wise. Surely, it would climb to a nickel or more before the end of the year, I told myself. The <u>Rollerball Cryptocurrency Hypothesis</u> had worked. If corporate power continued to increase, this seemed a good way to capitalize. It might take some time for the devolution of the nation-state, but it seemed like it could happen in the future.

On January 6th, 2021, I wondered if the future was NOW! As insurrectionists stormed the nation's Capitol, I watched in disbelief. I began to wonder if the election might be overturned or rerun. If Donald Trump walked down and stood at the Speaker's podium to state his case, he seemed capable of convincing enough people he was right to at last delay Biden taking power.

The existence of the Rollerball Cryptocurrency Hypothesis is proof positive of my active mind. I literally unable to turn off the machine. It is constantly gathering data and crunching information. It just IS for me.

Now as I watched the events of January 6th, I had to consider the possibility Donald Trump would walk down the street. His followers had secured the Capitol. He need only walk down the aisle and pick up the gavel. I watched a man in a buffalo head stand waiting for his leader to come to the podium.

What did this mean for America? What was actually going to happen. What did it mean for me? Would I take to the streets to oppose this anti-democratic action? I felt skeptical I would. Trump's whole presidency seemed to indicate the Republic was long dead.

As I considered the future, Donald Trump did not walk down the street. He did not take up the gavel as the man in the buffalo head had hoped. The insurrection was put down. Donald Trump backed away from the actions of his followers. Still, it was not clear to me afterwards that Joe Biden would be inaugurated.

Bezos was forced to get involved in politics in January. After the storming of the Capitol, there was a distinct air of insurrection in the air. There was not a lot of contrition from Trump and "his allies".

There was a growing social media effort to gather resources to disrupt the inauguration. Trump and others were booted from the prevailing social media platforms. The "rebels" were like an Internet slime though. They leaked through the closing fingers of a squeezing social media lock down.

Parler embraced the flood of downloads. They had more sign-ups than ever before. Apple and Google had stopped the downloads but it was too late. The Parler crowd had grown to a critical mass.

And then, something happened which changed the equation. As I considered the possibility of an "extended" Trump presidency after the election was declared invalid, one of the new factors needed to be weighted a bit more. I think Jeff Bezos got a little annoyed. He saw a real threat to the nation hosting his company. He took action to preserve the status quo which is so profitable for his corporation.

Jeff Bezos called down to the cloud services vice-president and suggested SOME aspect of the EULA had been violated by Parler. The vice-president agreed completely with Mr. Bezos' assessment. AWS stepped in and shutdown Parler.

The shutdown was hard and it was effective. It assured something which looked like a peaceful transition of power happened on January 20th, 2021. Jeff Bezos facilitated a peaceful transition of power. The economic stability provided by an autonomous corporate state was made crystal clear January 2021.

Frankly, the whole of the country probably owes Jeff Bezos a debt of gratitude for shutting down the insurrection. Now, Jeff Bezos is offering to use Amazon to assist with the vaccine distributions, too. Whether he likes it or not, an Amazon corporate state may be a necessity for economic stability in the United States. His company needs economic stability for it to continue to do business.

Jeff Bezos was a high profile target of some of the Trump Administration's tweets. The former president claimed Amazon was a monopoly and needed to be broken up. The Trump Administration did a high profile award to Microsoft of a coveted contract over Amazon. The former president appeared to have a personal beef, but Jess Bezos never weighed in directly.

Bezos seems to try to stay out of politics. One can presume he wants to avoid the corruption and the rancor of partisanship. He is an honest and earnest businessman and nothing else. At least that is what I think Jeff Bezos sees in the mirror.

Nonetheless, when he bought the Washington Post, he was dipping his toe into the swamp. He did seem to be pushing back a little on the Trump Administration attacks with this tool. Remember Bob Woodward works for Jeff Bezos now.

This is not a political statement. This is a fact. Retail investors can never ignore the hard facts. They are in such short supply.

Jeff Bezos embraces the America which allowed his company to grow to such a healthy size. The billionaire concentrates a good deal of money into Blue Origin. He keeps succeeding in this environment. A lot of the status quo favors Jeff Bezos.

Jeff Bezos is winning! Amazon was first to the cloud. AWS revenue is staggering but the business insight available to Amazon is even more mind-boggling. Any amount of stability in the status quo means Bezos continues to be winning.

The Accounts Receivable and Accounts Payable reports he has at his fingertips are a better indicator of the economic health of this nation than the S&P 500. There is a lot of money flowing through Amazon bank accounts at any moment. Jeff Bezos has the power to make many different things happen.

Bezos and his company have so much "currency" and has had it for so long, by default he has a great diversity of "currency" assets. He probably could start a banking empire based upon a digital currency overnight any time he chose. Jack Ma was on the cusp of doing just that when China brought him to heel.

The Post demonstrates Bezos understands "soft" power. Bezos controls a company of immense power and reach. Along with that there is this major media franchise with a strong investigative journalism arm at his disposal. By some measures, Amazon has more of the pieces in place for an autonomous corporate state than the aforementioned candidate in the <u>Rollerball Cryptocurrency Thesis</u>.

One of the most important things an autonomous power needs is an economic engine. They also need the power to keep things stable so business can be done. This is where I think Bezos has demonstrated the foundation for a corporate state already exists.

Perhaps this is the real reason Jeff Bezos has stepped down from the CEO position at Amazon. Many people speculate it is to pursue a political career. The lines of power are blurry. Future seems a bit foggy right now.

Would it be good or bad for cryptocurrency for there to be a President Bezos? It seems like it actually could be bad, because a President Bezos may want to shutdown competitors to his digital dollar initiative. That is what President Xi has done in China.

Cryptocurrency Investing is an Oxymoron

It must be clear now how uncertain I feel the future has become. This great uncertainty means everyone should be learning about cryptocurrency as a possible hedge against financial chaos. The current monetary system is in great flux this is true. However, the actual future system is a really unknown.

It is hard to know which cryptocurrency will really be the winner in the end. The nation-states will fight back through regulation and law. The nation states will not be above other coercion as Jack Ma learned. China may be able to control the cryptocurrency world in its borders with the digital remnibi.

The case for cryptocurrency investing as a hedge against unexpected financial upheaval makes sense in any case. It might make more sense for older people than younger ones. This might surprise the Bitcoin Bros on Reddit, but it is probably true. Younger people will have their lives to figure out how to adapt to the new realities. If you are old, there will be little time to adapt to wildly swinging circumstances which may occur.

Retirees may want to hedge to make sure they have something to fall back on. Smart retirees will prepare for the unexpected. Everyone wants their retirement years to be secure. When things are this uncertain wide diversification makes real sense.

Keep in mind though, such wide diversification indicates uncertainty. There are a wide number of outcomes. Some of those outcomes lead to some of those diversified assets going to zero while others may pay-off big.

The cryptocurrency universe is crazy…literally. Overnight there can be enormous moves in value, up AND down. It is why the term **"HODL"** caught on. A typo of "HOLD" became the acronym for **"Hold On** for **Dear Life"**.

Anyone holding Bitcoin over the last few years has ridden a roller coaster. It has gone from below $1000.00 to nearly $20,000.00. It was followed by a crash to something like $3000.00 in early 2020. At this writing, it is breaking past $50,000.00 in the Autumn of 2021.

The aforementioned is only a 20-month window of price swings on Bitcoin. Keep in mind Bitcoin is the most stable of the cryptocurrencies. This is just a small slice of what cryptocurrency investors go through trying to make and hold gains in the space.

There is a lot of work and intestinal fortitude required. Some crypto traders of course do not want to have their transactions reported to the IRS. They can have a good reason for this point of view. Regulatory guidance on cryptocurrency from the US government has been confusing.

It is not wrong to wait for regulatory clarity before putting one's cryptocurrency into the "system". However, it could be painful when the regulatory guidance does come. Every crypto investor has to make their own choices here. There has been talk of an 80% capital gains tax on cryptocurrency profits.

This space, the cryptocurrency space, is not heavily regulated…yet. Cryptocurrency investing is an oxymoron. It is straight up gambling given the amount of uncertainty around the space. There is so much complexity in the space. I find it difficult to recommend anyone diversify large amounts of their funds directly through an exchange.

I think a conservative person should think about using brokerage houses. These are more tightly regulated than the exchanges in the cryptocurrency world, like Binance or Kraken or Coinbase. There are ways to put money to work in cryptocurrency using the Wall Street infrastructure.

Yes, you will pay a premium for these investment vehicles. Nonetheless, you can now put money in the cryptocurrency space. The rules in cryptocurrency are being made up as I write. Do not forget there are numerous ne'er-do-wells looking to spear naive fortune seekers.

Some companies are seeing cryptocurrencies as a place to put their cash to work. These companies are doing the research for you. They have their normal business models but they also are doing cryptocurrency investing. Some companies have done so well in the cryptocurrency space, their traditional revenue streams may be eclipsed. Companies like MicroStrategy (MSTR) or Square (SQ) would be examples. Tesla recently announced putting over one billion dollars into Bitcoin.

Fortunately, you can easily sift through the companies with large cryptocurrency holdings. BitcoinTreasuries.org is a nice resource. Here you will find large Bitcoin holdings are documented. There are some ETFs in there if you visit the link. In fact, the largest single holder of Bitcoin listed at Bitcoin Treasuries is Grayscale Bitcoin Trust.

These are cryptocurrency ETF-like vehicles you can put money in. They have made it into the financial world. ETFs allow you to trade stock ticker symbols like you would GE,

CAT or AMZN. The ETFs are connected to the price of cryptocurrencies.

How exactly they are connected to the cryptocurrency price varies. Remember this is a lightly regulated space. You are abstracted away from the volatility. You pay a premium for this abstraction.

The nice thing is all the rules and regulations about the settlement of these transactions are in place. Buying these vehicles are like any regular stock market transactions. Grayscale has several investment vehicles that you can invest in. GBTC is the Bitcoin ETF and ETHE is the Ethereum vehicle Grayscale offers. There are others like the Litecoin Trust (LTCN). There are also diversified crypto vehicles as well.

Grayscale's vehicles even out the roller coaster ride for the average investor wishing to dip their toe into the cryptocurrency space. All the normal rules about the settlement will apply. When you decide you have had enough and want to get off the roller coaster, there will be a process. How you get your money is a well-worn path. This slightly more sane space for the retail investor.

Some of the readers are probably saying to themselves, but what about Robinhood? That seems like an easy way to buy cryptocurrencies at first glance. The fact that apps like Robinhood or PayPal do not even allow you to move the asset to a hardware wallet is not a favorable situation. Even though it feels like you can easily play the crypto space, these new apps tend to "freeze" during times of high volume. Because Robinhood is such a new entity, they are literally making up some of the rules as they go along. Those sudden rule changes rarely favor the retail investor.

Robinhood stock investors cannot even get out the door with their gains on a particular stock like Gamestop. The situation is even worse in the cryptocurrency world. If you ride the cryptocurrency rollercoaster in one of Robinhood's cars, you could get pitched out on a sudden downturn. Robinhood can get into a cash crunch at any particular time. History shows those times are most likely inconvenient ones for the retail investor.

The SEC is going to be looking closely at how Robinhood does business going forward after the "GameStonk" debacle. The idea of Robinhood empowering the retail investor is great but they themselves are too new at the game. There are other larger brokerage houses like TDAmeritrade, ETrade, or Schwab which have been doing business for decades. These players do not suffer Robinhood-like "hiccups".

Honestly my conscience requires me to suggest maybe you stop reading and start looking at those tickers. Perhaps put some money in play through your stock broker to wait and see. Cryptocurrency is a pretty complicated thing and it makes it an easy place to evaporate money.

There are people out there telling you all you want to hear about cryptocurrency investing. Most of them just want to get their hands on your 401K or other retirement nest egg. If you are committed to really understanding this new world of money then read on. You are going to need to get a hardware wallet.

Diving In and Getting a Hardware Wallet

I am not a fan of the term "cryptocurrency investing". Such a volatile, lightly regulated world where scammers outnumber legitimate experts a hundred to one is hardly an investing environment. There is so little regulation one must act like a medieval traveler constantly on the alert for highwaymen.

It is not just small independent scammers who are a threat in the cryptocurrency space. Robinhood is another bit of cognitive dissonance. Robinhood started in the stock market with commission-less trading. However, a closer look reveals the commissions can be rather high.

Paying for order flow, as Robinhood does, means they shop their customers orders around for the best profit for Robinhood. They are not seeking the best deal for their investor whose money they are using! Depending on the amount of money involved, the investor may very well have been better off paying a commission to a traditional broker.

Robinhood's cryptocurrency policy is even more one-sided and unfair. Robinhood is the actual holder of record of any cryptocurrency "purchased" by their clients. For the most part, Robinhood is simply selling interest in the future upside OR downside of any cryptocurrency it is already holding. That is it.

You cannot use the cryptocurrency you have at Robinhood. They promise someday to change this unfair situation. However, they have not done so as of this writing.

The exchanges like Binance, or Coinbase or Kraken, to name a few, are better options than Robinhood for sure. These entities make it easier to actually spend your cryptocurrency. Their wallet apps on a smartphone are quite sophisticated. It will take a while to jump through the identification hoops too. It hardly represents the instant gratification 21st-century people expect.

Additionally, exchange holders do not have the same control over their cryptocurrency on an exchange. If there is a run on cryptocurrency assets, getting trampled in the rush for the exits is a real problem. You could be stuck in a squeeze. It can hamstring your wealth when you are on another's platform. Worse yet, if an exchange gets hacked, there are no real guarantees. There is no FDIC to insure depositors. You are simply a victim with little recourse.

Finally, there is little to no anonymity on an exchange. These exchanges are able to operate within the United States because they follow the "Know Your Customer" rules closely. Dodging taxes is quite a gamble and illegal. Given the ambiguity of regulations in the cryptocurrency space, it makes sense to keep a low profile.

The regulations will come. Cryptocurrency has proven itself to be a threat to centralized control by bankers and nation states. To attempt to curtail this threat, one should expect regulations and taxes to be onerous. There is talk of an 80% capital gains tax put on cryptocurrency.

Cryptocurrency holders can be assured of one thing in this space. Whatever the government hands down, the exchanges will immediately cooperate. Governments make the rules. The exchanges have promised to comply. This is how they have been able to continue to operate.

However, one can enter the cryptocurrency universe without using an exchange. One should do so if one wants true control. Also, this path provides real privacy. The first step on this path would be obtaining a hardware wallet.

The Trezor hardware wallet is a good option and can be obtained at https://trezor.io for around $100. It is manufactured by Satoshi Labs. They were the first hardware wallet maker of any note and continue to lead the pack, in my opinion. The Nano Ledger and KeepKey are reasonable alternative hardware wallets, but I prefer the Trezor.

Hardware wallets are not cheap, but they are required. They are a necessity to exercise total control over the cryptocurrency of your choice. If you are feeling very smart, but are also feeling poor then you can build your own. If you want to save some money you can go to Pitrezor.com to check out a hardware wallet based on a Raspberry Pi.

Whichever wallet you choose, go to the vendor directly. Do not buy pre-configured wallets!!!! When you buy the wallet from the vendor, there will be a holographic seal on the wallet packaging. This seal assures the wallet has not been backed up onto the network with a private key.

The first time you hook up your hardware wallet to the vendor network, it will ask you if you want to back it up. I suggest not backing it up just yet. We are simply configuring now to hold a small amount of money. You can back up at any time. In fact, Trezor will nag you to do so every time you connect.

It is risky to not back up. One must understand the risks involved in this space. It is important to understand how easily things can get lost. Cryptocurrency was invented to be a new type of non-custodial asset.

For example, if a fifty dollar bill burns up, you are out of luck. This is how non-custodial assets work. Possession IS nine-tenths of the law. If someone has your fifty dollar bill or your lump of gold, you must prove it was stolen from you.

A hardware wallet without a backup key is completely secure because there is no backup to be rehydrated on the network. That is what the secret keys are all about. If you lose the hardware wallet, or run over it with your car or otherwise damage it, you can recreate it on a new piece of hardware. That is why it is so important to keep those keys to yourself.

With those keys, anyone can rehydrate the wallet. This rehydration is first come, first served. If the true owner asks the network to rehydrate onto a new piece of hardware, but the criminal has already done so, the rehydration will fail. Obtaining the private keys from a wallet is one of the most common scams in the cryptocurrency world. DO NOT GIVE YOUR PRIVATE KEYS TO ANYONE!

Cash is a non-custodial asset and so is cryptocurrency. In the case of a fifty dollar bill, the physical nature allows for better control of custody. You might lose it, but it will survive. If you run over it with your car or accidentally drop it in the water closet, the fifty dollar bill remains useful. A hardware wallet can get lost or broken or drowned in a toilet. It is not quite as durable as a fifty dollar bill.

The backup keys are just that a backup. The backup is also a security risk. Those keys give an individual the power to reach into your wallet to pluck the fifty dollar bill from your possession.

By starting without a back up, there will be heightened alertness, maybe a little thrill. I suggest doing it to help people truly get their brains around a new non-custodial asset like cryptocurrency. Of course, if you feel safer, go ahead and do the back up.

Do the backup to the hardware wallet vendor's network. This will generate a many word key, usually twenty-four words. You will be required to tediously go through all of these 24 words, at least twice during set up. Budget your time before continuing, it does take a little while.

Back up or do not backup, it is your decision. Remember you are the decision maker here. It is your money. It is enlightening to start out without backing up. Just put a small amount of cryptocurrency into the hardware wallet to start. Carrying around a fifty dollar bill has risk, but it can be fun to spend too.

In any case, with the hardware wallet of your choice configured and updated, you are ready. How are you going to get Bitcoin or other cryptocurrencies into that wallet?

You could buy it on an exchange after a tedious identity verification process or you could just "stick it into the wallet" like it was a fifty dollar bill.

If you are using a Trezor, go to wallet.trezor.io and generate an address using your computer. Bitcoin is the first in the list on the Trezor site, so find the tab for "Receive". This will generate an address for a Bitcoin transaction into your hardware wallet. A QR code will be presented along with a very long string of numbers and letters.

Simply take a photo of that QR code with your phone. The phone's AI will decode and show you the string of characters the QR image represents. I urge you to verify the string of characters on your phone versus the one on your computer screen to be double-dog sure you send your cryptocurrency to YOUR wallet.

Now all you need is to locate a Bitcoin ATM in your neighborhood. There are more than you think. Simply use a search engine like Google or DuckDuckGo and enter: "nearest Bitcoin ATM". You will be amazed by how many there are and where they are tucked away.

You can simply go to one of these ATMs, like CoinFlip or CoinHub to put money directly into your hardware wallet. Go to the machine with your smartphone in hand. This is the only identity most of these ATMs require. If you provide a mobile phone number, a name and perhaps an email address, you are good to go. The mobile phone has to work to receive texts. The rest of the information is on your honor. This surely beats the endless "Know Your Customer" merry-go-round. The waits when using an exchange can be interminable.

Once an ATM has located, visit it with your phone in hand. Leave your hardware wallet at home in a secure place. You will not need it at the ATM. Once in front of the machine, follow the prompts to identify yourself. You will be texted a code so you can move forward. Once you have put money into the machine, it will ask for the address of where you want it sent. Find the photo of your QR code and put it i front of the machine's electric eye. Click OK and Viola!

If you plan to hold, then dollar cost averaging via a Bitcoin ATM makes perfect sense. It certainly will allow you to wait for clearer regulations while still accumulating cryptocurrency privately. Dollar cost averaging will even out the inevitable volatility in the cryptocurrency world, too.

Most big cities in the United States have a few of these Bitcoin machines around. You can stand there and feed the machine fiat currency notes. You will identify yourself with a phone number and a Bitcoin wallet address.

All of these ATM networks will charge fees. I have found CoinFlip to be the most reasonable fees at around ten percent. I end up with $45 of Bitcoin in my hardware wallet after feeding the ATM a fifty dollar bill. Sometimes the transaction fees on the exchanges are way better, but not always. There is no doubt the exchanges can do better but not on the privacy front.

The ability to stay fairly anonymous via the ATM network has its attraction. Despite the fees, one can dollar cost average into the space. You can become a "crypto lurker" while waiting to see how regulation evolves.

In any case, once you have a little bit in the hardware wallet, spend it. Spend this new type of money, cryptocurrency. Have some fun with it. Buy yourself something. Nothing demonstrates the power of cryptocurrency like purchasing something with it.

As an earnest person and a father, I am writing the book about cryptocurrency as if one of my sons is going to read it. I am duty-bound to help the reader understand the new world of digital money which means detailing the dangers of the cryptocurrency world, too.

But before we do that, go buy something with your crypto! There are plenty of places which take cryptocurrency. If you are having problems finding a place to spend your crypto, try this site, https://thedogestore.co/. I know it is taking cryptocurrency because I helped write the code. LOL

Cryptocurrency Concerns

At the risk of beating a dead horse, I must stress as a cryptocurrency investor, you are really just a gambler. That is the truth. Do not ever forget it.

The central banks will fight back. The nation-states will fight back against decentralized financial systems. How this "fight back" evolves no one knows, but if Bitcoin were made illegal in the United States it is possible its valuation could crash.

The entire cryptocurrency universe is fraught with danger. It is hard to accept, but an outcome where Bitcoin or some other cryptocurrency ends up imploding to a price of zero is still possible. Anyone who is selling charts and analysis in cryptocurrency is selling snake oil.

Sure technical analysis can work sometimes in the cryptocurrency space until they do not work. At any point technical analysis might not work for very logical reasons. The cryptocurrency space is one crazy place with NO RULES!

The markets are not mature. There are large concentrations of holders, whales, who are able to pump or dump with the flip of a fluke. If you are on the wrong side of a whale's wake you will be capsized.

There is no real way to know what the whales (large crypto-holders) might do next.

There are many technical analysis models with a history of results in stock markets. Tools like Elliot Wave in mature well-capitalized markets make sense. In cryptocurrency, the concentrations of wealth by some big holders can move the market in directions Elliot Wave cannot predict. With concentrations of wealth, the action of one or two entities can move the market.

Also, remember there is not enough money on the planet to fund all the cryptocurrency being minted. Most of these currencies will die. They must. There are too many. If you are on a blockchain which shrivels up, it will be a sudden event. Everything happens on Internet time now. You will likely lose your entire investment. This universe is about gambling not about "investing".

Many people, especially, young people now believe the traditional markets are rigged. It is hard to argue, since Glass-Steagall's repeal. Its repeal allows the bankers of the United States to visit the global casino with their depositor's money.

The Federal Reserve is buying assets literally propping up the price of some companies. The Federal Reserve has made itself the backstop to a lot risky banking behavior. It makes sense young people do not see a difference between traditional markets and this new one.

Nonetheless, the fact traditional markets have become much less regulated is relative. These are only incremental steps toward further deregulation. The older market model is still more stable. It is still where most of the money is.

Where the money is, is where most of the power is. History tells us power rarely just gives up the reins voluntarily. The current banking oligarchy has power and they do not want to lose it. That is why you are hearing things like an 80% tax on cryptocurrency capital gains.

Imagine how it changes the calculus of your cryptocurrency investment when cashing out means you give most of it to the government. This is not without historical precedent. Remember, the **United States confiscated most of the privately held gold** within its borders during the Depression. This led quite directly to an attempted coup against Franklin Delano Roosevelt.

These are historical facts not paranoid delusions. The Business Plot was a political conspiracy in 1933 to overthrow the FDR presidency. A precious asset was pried from the citizenry and used to stabilize the nation's monetary system. This led the rich and powerful to push back and fund an unsuccessful coup. Those were "unprecedented times" in the Depression.

We are living in dangerous times and unprecedented things will happen. How does one calculate the risk related to the government simply taking most of your cryptocurrency investment gains? You cannot know when the agency will make the ruling or an executive order will come down.

This entire cryptocurrency world could be made illegal as the nation-states build their own digital currencies. They will not want private competitors so a whole host of cryptocurrency be made illegal. The risks here are HUGE AND INCALCULABLE. Cryptocurrency investing IS GAMBLING.

Texas Hold'em is gambling also. However, the game is structured such that one can play smartly. It does not mean one always wins because it is gambling, but one can increase one's odds by playing smart. In the crypto gambling world, Bitcoin is like Texas Hold'em, a less dangerous gamble, if you play your cards right.

I have now given you enough information to be dangerous. You can get out there and put some money in the game. It is a complicated world. There are scams everywhere. I have given you the safest and simplest path to play a hand in the cryptocurrency card game.

There are many other ways to invest in cryptocurrencies. There are staking plans which pay real dividends. There are arbitrage schemes which often yield big returns for those brave enough or smart enough to get wins.

I cannot encourage any of that behavior. We are all guessing here. Remember the term "Cryptocurrency Investing" is an oxymoron.

Appendix: Specific Cryptocurrencies

Bitcoin

Bitcoin is a digital currency that is underpinned by a kind of distributed ledger known as a "blockchain" running on a decentralized Proof of Work network. This ledger contains a record of all bitcoin transactions, arranged in sequential blocks. No user is allowed to spend any of their holdings twice. In order to prevent tampering, the ledger is public, or "distributed" to all the nodes on the network. An altered version of a block in the chain would quickly be rejected by other users so there is no need for a third-party validator of transactions, like a bank.

Unlike a fiat currency, Bitcoin has a capped supply. This cap is portrayed as if it is a law of the universe like gravity. This cap makes Bitcoin digital gold, we are told. There is a limited supply of Bitcoin like the precious metal, gold. Bitcoin's 21 million coin cap is currently built into the protocol.

This cap is approaching. The rewards for mining have been reduced significantly as far as the number of coins per "solve" of the Proof of Work equation. Because the price of Bitcoin has been increasing the reduced coin count has not seriously changed miner behavior.

No one actually knows what will happen when the cap is hit and no more Bitcoin will be rewarded for mining. The idea is that the network will be self-sustaining by this point. Transaction fees are expected to compensate node operators since mining will no longer yield coins.

However, it is also possible miners may flee the Bitcoin network for more lucrative currencies. Remember Bitcoin miners are humans. They do human-like things such as chasing returns. On the other hand, the transaction fees may more than suffice to retain miners and hold the 21 million coin cap.

If miners did flee, however, it could be a big problem for the Bitcoin network. This would harm the network and make the dreaded 51% attack more possible. It is also possible the Bitcoin protocol will be changed to allow for more than 21 million coins to retain the miners and harden the network.

This is possible. Code can be changed. One wonders what might happen to BTC value if this happened. Remember changing code is a lot easier than digging stuff out of the ground. There is a mechanism for changing the code as bugs appear occasionally and MUST be fixed.

What? You did not realize the Bitcoin code could just be changed to allow for more coins. You thought all this stuff Satoshi put together was immutable and unchangeable. The truth is no one actually knows what will happen as the cap approaches. That is why Cryptocurrency Investing is an Oxymoron and many smart people will argue that the 21 million coin cap is completely and utterly unchangeable.

Ethereum

If the analogy of a 'distributed ledger' to describe Bitcoin seems complicated, Ethereum is magnitudes more complex. Sure a Proof of Work blockchain enables a decentralized currency because of the rules which govern what one can and cannot do to modify the ledger. For example, a Bitcoin address cannot spend more Bitcoin than it has previously received. These rules underpin all transactions on cryptocurrency blockchains.

Ethereum has a native cryptocurrency (Ether) that follows almost exactly the same intuitive rules. However, there is no real cap on Ether right now and likely this situation will persist. Ether also enables the new and much more powerful function of smart contracts which drives Fintech. Instead of a distributed ledger,

Ethereum is a distributed state machine supporting DeFi apps and many others.

The Ethereum Virtual Machine manages all of this complexity. It is all very cool. Too cool really, because so many smart contract applications are now built on this blockchain, it is often painfully slow or prohibitively expensive to get things done.

For this reason and many others real and imagined, a new version of Ethereum is scheduled to come out soon. Ethereum 2.0 promises a new model, Proof of Stake, which will be more environmentally friendly and faster than Ethereum as it stands. Whether this will happen is still open to speculation because the miners must cooperate or a hard fork could occur. As of this writing, Ethereum 2.0 remains a gleam in Vitalik Buterin's eye.

Litecoin

LTC is the cryptocurrency world's ultimate wallflower. Litecoin never seems to get any love. Nonetheless, it is one of the oldest cryptocurrencies as It continues to exist and perform actual duties. It is one of the most well-known and trusted cryptos out there.

Litecoin is a robust cryptocurrency like Bitcoin. It is fully decentralized and boasts a healthy miner ecosystem. It has been consistent in the market cap's top 10 since its inception in 2011. It is widely used globally. Yes, people really use Litecoin. Yet, Litecoin gets very little press.

The Litecoin network has zero downtime and 100% uptime. It is a true proof of work currency. On any given day, it is transacting over a billion dollars. Despite the usage, it is still fast to transfer money and extremely cheap compared to other financial protocols.

Litecoin's inventor, Charlie Lee, wanted to create digital silver to supplement the digital gold which Bitcoin represents. Like Bitcoin, Litecoin also has a supply limit. Litecoin has four times the supply of Bitcoin. Bitcoin's supply is capped at 21 million, which means that Litecoin has a supply limit of 84 million coins.

Charlie Lee created Litecoin in 2011 by tweaking Bitcoin's code while working at Google. He then served as director of engineering at the crypto exchange Coinbase Inc. Coinbase listed Litecoin while Lee was still on the payroll, which would seem to violate some rule somewhere, but it is the Wild West people! in any case, Lee left soon after the listing to focus on Litecoin.

Later the inventor bailed out. Lee announced his decision on Dec. 20, 2017, when he sold almost all of his coins into the market. Since that time, Litecoin has lost favor though not utility. It is hard to blame Lee. In the crypto world, money can be lost in large volumes. Losers of enormous amounts of money often look for someone to blame.

Litecoin has a real-world use case in the payment domain already extant. With Litecard, payments are even easier. Litecoin has over 50,000 transactions on the network per day. Litecoin is one of the most liquid and stable cryptocurrencies without actually being a stable coin. Litecoin is on just about every exchange, so whether the inventor has a big stake or not no longer really matters.

Dogecoin

There is a cryptocurrency out there that many consider a joke. That cryptocurrency is Dogecoin. One can be excused for thinking this since the cryptocurrency was created literally as a joke. As such the value of the coin has historically been in fractions of a penny.

Dogecoin was created by Jackson Palmer and Billy Markus to satirize the growth of altcoins by making the doge internet meme into a cryptocurrency. It is a derivative of Luckycoin which forked from Litecoin and uses a Scrypt algorithm.

Dogecoin started its initial coin production schedule with 100 billion coins in circulation. By mid-2015 the 100 billionth Dogecoin had been mined though. Now, an additional 5 billion coins are put into circulation every year.

There is no cap to the supply of coins and thus the coin can inflate infinitely. Dogecoin had a supply limit of 100 billion coins, which when launched was far more coins than the top digital currencies were allowing. Nonetheless, by February 2014, Dogecoin founder Jackson Palmer removed the limit. He announced there would be no cap.

This cap removal was partially to continue the joke. Bitcoin and other cryptocurrencies do have a cap on the number of coins the system will support. Dogecoin without a cap should suffer from a constant reduction of its value over time. It is years later though. The Shiba Inu is still grinning and Dogecoin well above fractions of a penny. This is a significant increase over its historically low price.

It got so hot now I saw Dogecoin charts on CNBC and Bloomberg. I heard commentators stumble over 'Dogecoin' on the teleprompter. It might be Dog-E-coin at first, then they call it Dodge-coin followed by Dough-ja-coin. Then they grin thinking they finally got it right!

I admit that in my head, I always call it DoggyCoin, because the first time I saw it, I thought the meme was cute. I like cute doggies, but that is not the correct way to say the world's favorite cryptocurrency's name. I try to purge that Doggy word from my mind, but then I will stumble. Sometimes I will say "Dojah"coin. Maybe I think this sounds like I have some street cred, like Sister Soulja. I am not sure why this tongue slip occurs

Well here is how to pronounce Dogecoin. One of the inventors confirms it is "DOhj"coin. They were Japanophiles. The name is made up but "sounds" Japanese. Their chosen mascot is the Shiba Inu. It is pronounced DO-long O and then the G is a kind of soft J sound, then the E is completely silent... "dohj"coin -> #dogecoin.

There you go. You now know how to pronounce the cutest cryptocurrency around. Dogecoin will always be DoggyCoin to me, but it may not remain a Proof of Work cryptocurrency, though. Vitalik Buterin appears to have been brought in by Elon Musk to move this cryptocurrency to some kind of staking model. As it stands though, Dogecoin is mined and validated by the Litecoin miners and that decentralized network.

Monero

Bitcoin is a public blockchain. Everyone can look and see addresses and validate the ledger. Monero is the cryptocurrency to use when you NEED things to be private.

Unlike Bitcoin, you don't receive funds at your public address. Instead, Monero places the funds in a new anonymous account and then locks that account with a password only you can discover. This way your Monero is never associated with your public address.

Every transaction on Monero involves creating one of these new anonymous accounts. Monero calls these new accounts stealth addresses. The stealth address creates a layer of anonymity between the public address and the Monero owned. The addresses on the publicly available blockchain are stealth, so personally identifiable information stays off the blockchain.

Monero's privacy algorithm is formidable. That is why there is a bounty on Monero's head with the IRS offering a reward for cracking its privacy algorithm. Monero remains a Proof of Work cryptocurrency, but one wonders whether the central government's regulatory agencies will allow it to remain legal.

www.ingramcontent.com/pod-product-compliance
Lightning Source LLC
Chambersburg PA
CBHW071516220526
45472CB00003B/1042